11-04

MODERN WORLD NATIONS

MODERN WORLD NATIONS

Scotland

Roger Dendinger
South Dakota School of
Mines and Technology

Series Consulting Editor
Charles F. Gritzner
South Dakota State University

Chelsea House Publishers

Frontispiece: Flag of Scotland

Cover: A stone bridge provides access to a castle at the edge of a loch. Highlands, Scotland.

CHELSEA HOUSE PUBLISHERS

EDITOR IN CHIEF Sally Cheney
DIRECTOR OF PRODUCTION Kim Shinners
CREATIVE MANAGER Takeshi Takahashi
MANUFACTURING MANAGER Diann Grasse

Staff for SCOTLAND

EDITOR Lee Marcott
PRODUCTION ASSISTANT Jaimie Winkler
PICTURE RESEARCH 21st Century Publishing and Communications, Inc.
COVER AND SERIES DESIGNER Takeshi Takahashi
LAYOUT 21st Century Publishing and Communications, Inc.

http://www.chelseahouse.com

First Printing

1 3 5 7 9 8 6 4 2

Library of Congress Cataloging-in-Publication Data

Dendinger, Roger.
  Scotland / Roger Dendinger.
     p. cm. — (Modern world nations)
Summary: A look at the geographic, political, economic, and social
aspects of Scotland, a country with ancient traditions that also plays a
major role in the economy of present-day Europe.
Includes bibliographical references (p.   ) and index.
  ISBN 0-7910-6782-3
  1. Scotland—Juvenile literature. [1. Scotland.] I. Title. II.
Series.
  DA762 .D46 2002
  941.1—dc21

                          2002003534

Table of Contents

Scotland

Piper at Eilean Donan Castle, Loch Duich, Highland Region.

1

Introducing Scotland

Any short list of the world's most famous cultures would surely include Scotland. The Scots accent, the Scots kilt, tartans, bagpipes, and Scotch whiskey are known the world over. Famous for retaining its traditional customs and folkways, Scotland is also well-known as a place where history and modernity coexist side by side. The country that gave the world "Auld Lang Syne," the ultimate in sentimental songs, is also the country that produces half of all laptop computers sold in Europe.

Any list of the world's most romantic landscapes would likewise include Scotland. Its hills and mysterious lochs—one containing a fabled monster—are the stuff of song, poetry, fiction, and folktale. A land of coastlines and lonely islands where no place is far from the ocean, Scotland has attracted adventurous people for millennia: the pre-Celtic Stone-Age folk who came by land during the last great ice age, various Celtic tribes, the Britons and the Scots, Roman legionnaires, and Viking raiders from Norway and Denmark. All came to explore, conquer, and settle the northern portion of the island of Britain, a land so close in space yet so different in atmosphere from the south. Attracted by the long sea inlets into the island's interior and by the proximity to northern European coasts, the various peoples of ancient Scotland all left traces of their lives on the land and contributed to the rich heritage of the Scottish nation.

But Scotland is more than a romantic idyll, more than a land of past wonders and poetic glory. It is also a country where invention and economic adaptability have a long tradition. In the Scotland of the 21st century, the old cottage industry of weaving world-famous Harris tweeds is still practiced in the Western Isles (also known as the Hebrides). At the same time, in the midsection of the country, one of the world's fastest growing software development centers is growing in Glasgow's "Silicon Glen." High tech and Highland craft are equally at home in this new Scotland.

Long a valued partner in empire with England, Scotland has also long chafed at its junior role in the United Kingdom. Always aware and proud of its separate identity as a nation, it now seeks greater independence. A revival of ancient national pride is moving Scotland into an exciting new century and a new expression of nationhood in a broader economic and political context. As Europe forges a new regional identity for itself with the supranational organization known as the European Union, Scotland is moving to take its place within this new political and economic association. So we may also consider Scotland as a land of political contradiction. While it moves to set itself apart politically once again from its larger English neighbor, it is also moving to join a greater political association. Devolution and supranationalism are both important political aspects of the new Scotland.

Scotland has long been allied with the United States and

Loch Beinn at Glen Affrie, Highland Region.

Canada. Many Scots immigrated to the U.S. in the 19th and 20th centuries. Scottish ethnicity is now a source of great pride for hundreds of thousands of U.S. citizens. Annual "gatherings of the clans" are held from the Southern Appalachian Mountains of North Carolina to the Black Hills of South Dakota. From California to New York, Americans celebrate

Located off the northwest coast of Europe, two countries occupy the British Isles: the Republic of Ireland and the larger United Kingdom of Great Britain and Northern Ireland. The United Kingdom incorporates the island of Great Britain, consisting of England, Scotland, Wales, the northeastern corner of Ireland, and most of the smaller out-islands. As Europe forges a new identity as the European Union, Scotland is moving to take its place within this new political and economical association.

their ancestral connections to the old country of Scotland. According to one Scottish ancestry organization, more than 300 clan events and Celtic festivals are held each year in North America. This connection makes Scotland a country of enduring interest for many Americans. The cultural ties and friendly relations between the two countries are expressed in the growing number of U.S.-based transnational corporations that have invested in Scotland. U.S. companies produce everything from clothing to photographic equipment, semiconductors, and telecommunications products in Scotland.

A look at the new Scotland begins with a look at the land. Scotland's natural landscape provides the setting, the stage set, for the long evolution of the cultural strengths of the Scottish nation and what promises to be a return to the independence of the Scottish state.

Boats in a Scottish harbor. Much of the west coast of Scotland is a wild,
deeply indented mountain wall. The east coast also includes long stretches
of steep cliffs broken up by extensive stretches of long sandy coast.

Natural
Landscapes

I f you are a beachcombing visitor to the Hebrides Islands or Scotland's western coast, you might be surprised by what the sea offers up in the way of beach treasures. The westerly wind drift drives the warm waters of the Gulf Stream off the southeastern United States all the way north to the British Isles. Called the North Atlantic drift, this combination of wind and water fetches driftwood from the Caribbean and flotsam from the Carolinas up to Scottish beaches to startle visitors and long-time beachcombers alike.

Despite its position in the northern latitudes—between 54 and 60 degrees north—Scotland's climate is temperate. In fact, Scotland is a perfect example of the climate type known as "marine west coast"—climates that are relatively warm with mild winters and sufficient rainfall year-round. Along with the Gulf

Stream's warm waters from the southwest come relatively warm west winds that moderate both winter and summer temperatures. Summers are comfortably cool, and winters, although often cold, are seldom harsh. In fact, Scotland's winter season is warmer than other northern European regions at similar latitudes, such as southern Norway or Denmark. No average air temperature for any location falls below freezing any time during the winter, making Scottish winters similar to those of Belgium or the Netherlands.

Rainfall throughout the country averages 22 to 40 inches (about 0.5 to 1 meter) annually. The west, particularly the Highlands, tends to receive more rain than the east. Aberdeen and Dundee, two of the larger cities on the east coast, receive 31 inches (0.8 meter) on average.

From its northern tip to its southern border with England, Scotland is only 275 miles (443 kilometers) long, and its maximum width is only 154 miles (248 kilometers). Few places in Scotland are more than 40 miles (64 kilometers) from the Atlantic Ocean or the North Sea. So indented is the coastline with long sea inlets that its estimated aggregate length is 2,300 miles (3,700 kilometers).

The physical setting of Scotland lends itself to a neat three-part division of the country: the Highlands, the Lowlands, and the Southern Uplands.

The northern two-thirds of the island of Britain is known as the Highlands, a name used for over a thousand years to distinguish the wild north region from the lower elevations of the south. The Highlands region lies northwest of a line between Stonehaven on the east coast and Dumbarton near the head of the Firth of Clyde in the west. All of this northern territory is considered part of the Highlands, except Caithness in the extreme northeastern peninsula and low-lying coastal areas of the east from Banff south to the Firth of Forth. The Hebrides Islands and the other western isles are usually considered part of the

Hikers descend the icy summit of Ben Nevis, the highest mountain in Great Britain at 4,406 feet. Ben Nevis, in the Grampians, is located at the highest point of the Highlands in Scotland.

Highlands, although the northern island groups, the Orkneys and Shetlands, are not.

The Grampian Hills are the highest parts of the Highlands, and the highest mountain elevation in all of Great Britain is located in the Grampians: Ben Nevis, at 4,406 feet (1,343 meters). Five other peaks over 4,000 feet (1,219 meters) are located in the Grampians. These are not high mountains by European Alpine standards, but the beauty of the Scottish mountains is unmatched. Long a destination for hiking enthusiasts from the south, the hill ranges of the Highlands have a unique appeal. Heavily deforested over several millennia of human occupation, the hills and rolling uplands are being replanted and reclaimed as hunting and natural reserves. Experts believe that most of the heaths, hilly undulating plains, and heather- and juniper-covered moors in Scotland and in the rest of Britain were human induced. Fire was used by the Celts to clear land later used by the Scots as pasturelands. Today, extensive reforestation projects are turning old sheep pastures into new forests of spruce and fir.

Scotland's emblematic natural landscapes are found in the Highlands. Many of the long inlets—or firths—that punctuate Scotland's coastline are found in the north as are the famous lochs, the deep and beautifully narrow Scottish lakes. The biggest, Loch Lomond, covers more than 27 square miles (70 square kilometers) and has a maximum depth of 623 feet (190 meters). The setting for many poems and tales of the Highlands, Loch Lomond is immortalized in the well-known 18th-century song:

Oh ye'll take the high road
and I'll take the low road,
An' I'll be in Scotland before ye',
But wae is my heart until we meet again
On the bonnie, bonnie banks
O' Loch Lomond.

Heather and trees on the banks of Loch Lomond, a lake which has been the setting for many poems and tales of the Highlands.

By far the most famous of Highland lochs—and the deepest, at 754 feet (227 meters)—is Loch Ness, home of the rarely seen monster Nessie. Sonar surveys of the loch routinely fail to provide any evidence of the monster, but believers point out that such surveys also fail to prove that she doesn't exist. Regardless of Nessie's reality, the beauty and mystery of Loch Ness continue to attract tourists from around the world.

The Hebrides, also known as the Western Isles, are part of the Highland region. The Hebrides are divided between the Outer (Lewis, Harris, the Uists) and Inner isles (Skye, Mull, Islay). Over 700 other islands crowd the waters off Scotland's shores. Many are small, uninhabited rocks, but about 130 are inhabited. Most of Scotland's island population lives either in the Hebrides or in the two northern archipelagos, the Orkneys and the Shetlands—the northernmost portion of Scottish territory.

The southern Grampians mark a natural boundary between the Highlands and the narrow waist of Scotland. This region, the Central Lowlands, includes the valleys of the Clyde, Tay, and Forth Rivers. Between the Firths of Clyde and Forth, Scotland is only 25 miles wide.

Despite its name, the Lowlands is a region of low rolling hills and farmlands. Located here are the famous Coal Measures, the coalfields and iron ores that lie in a narrow belt from the head of the Firth of Clyde in the west across to the Firth of Forth. This was the center of Scotland's early industrial development and is still the most densely pop-ulated portion of the country. The world-famous dairy-cow breed the Ayrshire originated in the county of the same name in the west Lowlands.

The southern Lowlands boundary is a line from coastal Girvan on the west to Dunbar at the mouth of the Firth of Forth. South of this line lies the third major region of Scotland, the Southern Uplands. Seven low ranges of hills

The bridge over the Firth of Forth in Queensferry, Scotland, was constructed in 1890.

with elevations up to 2,700 feet (823 meters) distinguish this area. The famous Cheviot Hills and the Tweed River on the 60-mile (97 kilometers) English border are landmarks. This is Sir Walter Scott country, the Scottish Borderlands, famous in legend and song. Richer in soil fertility than other parts of

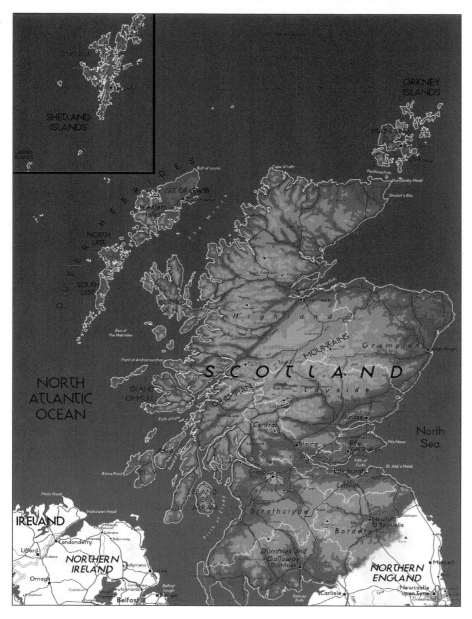

The map of Scotland shows the highlands and lowlands and the large number of out-
islands that make up the country. The Scottish Lowlands compose only about one-fifth
of the land area of Scotland, but this is where four-fifths of the population live. The two
main cities of Glasgow on the west and Edinburgh on the east are in the lowlands. The
Scottish Highlands are low mountains—Ben Nevis is the highest at 4,406 feet—but many
slopes are steep and seem higher because they rise from a base at or near sea level.

the country, the Uplands contain some of Scotland's most prized landscapes. Being closest to England, it is the most Anglicized part of the country. For centuries it has been the natural borderland separating the northern people of the island of Britain from their southern neighbors.

The Callenish Standing Stones on the Outer Hebridean island of Lewis.
Dated from 4,000 years ago, the site consists of over 50 standing stones,
arranged in the form of a Celtic Cross.

Scotland Through Time

I n Scotland, history is writ in stone. The first human settlers were Stone Age people who migrated to the coasts and islands about 6,000 years ago. We know this first great stretch of Scottish prehistory primarily from the large irregular blocks of stone used for ritual construction by these first people. These stones, or megaliths, provide dramatic evidence of a mysterious prehistoric past whose ancient inhabitants left traces of their culture in the form of great stone circles. These are found from the Outer Hebrides to the Firth of Clyde in the south. Scattered across the land are Neolithic (late Stone Age) chamber tombs and mysterious Bronze Age (3500–1000 B.C.) stone circles, such as the one at Callenish on the Isle of Lewis.

Among the most distinctive megalithic structures are the "standing stones," single upended blocks, or, more commonly, groups or alignments of stones standing on end. On the western isles, many standing stones dot the lonely windswept shores. Other megalith structures are associated with burials. The Loch Ness megaliths include an elaborate cairn with an alignment toward the midwinter sunset, surrounded by standing-stone formations. From Caithness in the far northeast to the Kilmartin valley in the southeast near the Firth of Clyde, megaliths are stark memorials to the ancient inhabitants who marked their land in stone.

Spanning thousands of years of human habitation, these remains hint at a harsh life of raiding and warfare. Many vestiges of defensive architecture, such as wheelhouses (stone houses built in the shape of a circle with walls projecting inward like spokes of a wheel) and brochs (circular double-walled towers with central courtyards) dot the land. The Broch of Mousa on Shetland is a well-preserved example. But researchers also find evidence of a rich spiritual culture. From gravesites, archeologists piece together bits of an ancient religion that included an elaborate conception of a spiritual afterlife. Grave goods were sometimes lavish, indicating a strong belief in immortality. The origins of these first people are still unknown, but their presence lingers in stone from one end of Scotland to the other.

Much nearer to our own time are works in stone that mark the beginning of Scotland's recorded history. These are the great engineering feats of the Roman Empire, Hadrian's Wall and Antonine's Wall. Although the Romans explored the southeastern coast of Scotland as far north as the mouth of the Tay River in 79 A.D., it was more than 40 years later that the Roman legions advanced north to the region now known as the Borderlands. Here they met fierce warrior tribes who checked their march north. South of what is now the border with England, the Romans built Hadrian's Wall as a frontier outpost to contain these people. Known to the Romans as Caledonii, these Pictish tribes inhabited the

The ruins of an ancient Stone-Age village that was built ca. 2000-1500 B.C. lay along the coastline of Skara Brae, Orkney Islands.

northern portion of the island of Britain. The Romans called this northern land Caledonia. Today, this is still the poetic name for Scotland.

Hadrian's Wall was constructed in 127 A.D., several years after Emperor Hadrian visited this far-flung outpost of his empire. Some 80 Roman miles long (73 modern miles/117 kilometers), in places 15 feet (4.6 meters) high, built of stone and turf, the wall was punctuated by a series of milecastles, guard towers manned by Roman legionnaires. North of this first wall is the high-water mark of the Roman occupation of the island and the farthest northern extent of their European empire: Antonine's Wall, built in 143 A.D. This 35-mile (56-kilometer) fortification linked the estuaries of the Firth of Forth and the Firth of Clyde. Built to imperial Rome's high engineering standards across the narrow waist of Scotland, this wall successfully separated Roman-occupied Britain from the barbarians of the north. After a few years, however, relentless attacks from the Picts forced the Romans to retreat to their earlier fortifications in the south. Hundreds of years after the Romans abandoned their northern outpost, stones from the walls and fortifications were used in another kind of wall construction when Scottish farmers took the old Roman stones as ready-made blocks for building cottages and fences.

Among the various peoples who came to the land known as Scotland, the Romans—unlike the pre-Celts, the Picts, and later, the Vikings—were not settlers but conquerors, administrators, governors. Their cultural contribution to the island of Britain was primarily in the built environment. They left behind roads, walls, fortifications, baths, and toponyms, or place-names, including the name Britain itself, derived from *Britoni,* the Roman version of what the Celts called themselves: Pretani. The Roman legacy in Scotland also includes Christianity, which came to the island with the Roman legions in the last 100 years of their occupation.

The Romans pulled their last legions out of Britain in 407 A.D. As the Romans abandoned their walls and towns that had been built from Scotland's ancient stones, new invaders came. A Celtic people, the Gaels, sailed across the narrow North Channel of the Irish Sea from the northeast corner of Hibernia. Called Scotti, or Scots, by the Romans, the Gaels began arriving in the fifth century and were initially

Hadrian's Wall, Northumberland, Northern England, was constructed in 127 A.D. by the Romans to contain fierce warrior tribes to the north.

resisted by the Picts. By about 500 A.D. they had established themselves in coastal villages and strongholds along Britain's northwest, where they fought with the Picts off and on for the next several centuries. With the conversion of Pictish kings to Christianity, hostility between Scots and Picts gradually subsided.

In the eighth century another wave of invasions began. From Norway and Denmark came the Vikings, or Norsemen. The earliest recorded Viking raids were in 795. After a few years of coastal marauding, however, the Vikings shifted from raiding to settling Scotland. The first permanently inhabited fortified villages began as raiding bases. By 900, Norwegian Vikings had established themselves in the islands and along the coast from Galloway to Moray Firth. The Norse invaders largely submerged the Celts of the Orkney and Shetland Islands, but in the Hebrides and in the southwest, the Scottish Celts intermarried with the Norsemen. These people were known to the Irish as the Gall-Gaedhil ("foreign Gael"), from which present-day Galloway gets its name. The Norse invaders left many other place-names on the landscape of Scotland. Today hundreds of toponyms, mostly island and coastal place-names, reflect Scotland's Viking heritage. Among other formations, place-name suffixes often indicate Viking influence or origins. For example, the "-ey" ending in names for Britain's northern islands, the Orkneys derives from the old Norse term for island.

The Vikings broke the existing piecemeal territorial power structure of post-Roman Scotland. A century after the Roman retreat, a cultural pattern had emerged based on four ethnic territories. The Pict tribes controlled most of the Highlands, the Scots held the western highlands, the Britons occupied Strathclyde in the south, and the Angles lived in the southeast. All four of these groups suffered from Viking raids, but the Scots suffered the least. From their power base in the west, they gradually extended control over the other groups and their lands. The Picts were largely overcome by 844; the Britons were absorbed around 900, and the Angles in 973. Gradually adding bits of territory to what became the kingdom of Scotland, the Scots and Picts were formally united in 843 by Kenneth MacAlpin, the first ruler of the land known as Alba, Scotland's Gaelic name. Alba at this time consisted of most of the territory north of the Firths of Forth and Clyde. Although Vikings traded, invaded, and settled throughout the British Isles, their influence remained longest in Scotland. One important region not included in the kingdom of Scotland until much later was the northern and western islands. The Hebrides remained part of the Viking kingdom centered on the Isle of Man until the 13th century. The Shetlands and Orkneys were both Norse dependencies until 1472.

Shortly after Alba's unification, the long struggle to remain independent from its larger southern neighbor began. After coming under English control in the 12th century, Scotland reaffirmed its independence by defeating the English at the battle of Bannockburn in 1314. From then until 1688 the House of Stuart ruled Scotland. During this same period, Scotland was more closely associated with mainland Europe than with England. Trade flourished with Scandinavia, the Netherlands, and the Baltic region. The "Auld Alliance" with France united Scotland with England's major competitor on the mainland and forged one of Europe's most enduring national friendships. For generations, kings of France recruited their personal bodyguards from the Scottish military.

Centuries of economic and political stalemate with England ended with the Act of Union in 1706. The act dissolved the Scottish parliament on May 1, 1707, and decreed that thereafter England and Scotland would be ruled by one united parliament in London. Many Scots believe that the Act of Union was the result of economic coercion by the English. Writing many years later, the great Scottish poet Robert Burns identified the economic motives of the union: "We are bought and sold for English gold/ Such a parcel o' rogues in a nation." Events leading up to the act bear out the economic explanation.

In the 1660s England restricted access to its valuable North American colonies with a series of laws. The Navigation Acts required that trade with English colonies be conducted by

This illustration, dated 1794, shows Edward I in Parliament. Seated on Edward's right is Alexander III, King of Scotland, and on his left, Llywelyn ap Gruffudd, Prince of Wales.

English ships docking in English ports. Since much Scottish trade at this time was with colonies in North America, the national economy slowed drastically. Scotland responded by attempting its own colony in the New World—the Darien expedition of 1696—but this failed quickly and nearly drove the government into bankruptcy. Scottish landowners and investors believed that uniting with their southern rival was the only way out of their economic dilemma.

The Act of Union dissolved the Scottish parliament and brought Scotland firmly under the political control of England. Shortly after, however, Scotland's international trade boomed, so much so that Scottish merchants quickly came to dominate the lucrative market in tobacco and to invest heavily in other North American exports to Europe. The Scottish merchant navy grew from fewer than 100 ships in 1700 to 2,000 in 1800. The economic revival turned out to be to the mutual advantage of both Scotland and England. Scotland's 18th-century wealth made it a valuable junior partner in the burgeoning world empire being forged by England.

The growth of that empire was fueled by the scientific and industrial developments known as the Industrial Revolution. Rural areas, rather than cities, saw the first waves of industrialization, which took place in textile manufacturing. Located wherever waterfalls and rapids could power machine looms, new factories appeared in the north of England and in the Scottish Lowlands. The water-powered textile boom of the early 18th century was followed by other waves of Scottish development that mirrored England's industrial growth. Steel, steam, and shipbuilding were all important Scottish contributions to the industrialization of the UK and the world.

In 1709 coke, which was a cheap residue of coal, was substituted for charcoal in smelting, and steelmaking became cheaper. Steelmaking was relocated to coal districts where coke could be obtained easily. The western Scottish Lowlands are rich in coal, and this area became the premier industrial center of the country. In an age driven largely by steam power, the Scot James Watt developed the governor, the condenser, and the crank, creating the world's first powerful industrial steam engines. Another native of Scotland, William Symington, built the engine for the world's first steamboat. As steelmaking was refined, the Clydeside district near Glasgow grew to be one of the world's most important shipbuilding centers. Close to coal, steel mills, and navigable waterways, Clydeside came to dominate British shipbuilding for most of the 19th and 20th centuries. By 1890 the UK was producing about 80 percent of the world's seagoing tonnage, much of it in Glasgow. Clydeside shipbuilding peaked in 1913 and slowly declined in the face of foreign competition.

After the Act of Union and Scotland's 18th century economic and industrial boom, competition for land became a major force changing the traditional culture of the Highlands. Land tenure before the Act of Union was based on the old Scottish clan system of dispersed farmsteads. Each clan chief leased land out to *tacksmen,* who in turn rented parcels to tenant farmers. Under this traditional system no one clearly "owned" land in the conventional sense. This land distribution system was recognized by monarchs and clan chiefs until after the Act of Union. In the 1740s the UK Parliament passed laws that profoundly affected Scottish lands. The Heritable Jurisdictions Act extended English jurisdiction to all Highland landowners, making the old clan chiefs the owners—on paper—of clan lands. This sparked an exodus of landowners to London. Beginning in the 1760s landowners begin raising rents, installing fences, and removing thousands of tenants to clear land for sheep. The new textile factories in the Lowlands and in England were hungry for wool as demand for new machine-made textiles increased. The era known as the Clearances, or the Highland Removals, had begun.

Small farms in Scotland are known as crofts; the farmers who rent the land are crofters. Forcibly removing crofters and their families—and sometimes entire villages—from their lands, landlords displaced thousands of Highlanders. Many of the dispossessed were sent to Canada. Others migrated to the U.S. and, later, to Australia. From 1770 to 1790 more than 6,400 crofters emigrated from the Inverness area alone. Clearances were often marked by violence. Owners would sometimes come at night, driving people from their cottages

By 1890 the United Kingdom was producing most of the seagoing ships and much of this work was done in Scotland. Here, the huge turbine engines are being put on board the *Aquitania* at the shipyards in Clydebank.

and burning the dwellings so that they had no place to live. Over time, the burning of crofter's cottages and farm buildings became a common practice. Some crofters responded with violence of their own. Complicating the problems of the Highlanders, in 1845 the potato blight wiped out most of the potato harvest, sparking the migration of thousands of people to the rapidly growing urban areas of Britain and to

A group of islanders make their way to the pier at Lochboisdale, Outer Hebrides, to board a Canadian ferry. Some 300 inhabitants of the Hebridian islands emigrated to Canada in 1924 after the collapse of foreign fish markets and harsh weather conditions.

the U.S. In the 1850s more violent removals occurred. In one infamous case—the 1851 clearance of Barra— Colonel Gordon, the landlord, called a meeting of his tenant farmers, threatening them with fines if they didn't attend. Almost 1,500 of them arrived at the meeting place, where they were seized, bound, and taken to ships headed for America.

The troubles of those times are not yet forgotten. In 1994 local residents in a northern town tried unsuccessfully to get a

27-foot-high (8 meters) statue of the Duke of Sutherland—one of the worst landlords of the clearances era—taken down from a prominent overlook in town. Rather than removing the statue, the local government constructed a series of public history information plaques describing the hardships caused by the clearances.

Some creative solutions to land ownership in the Highlands have been found. In 1996 the landlord of one large estate on the Kyle of Tongue set up a free transfer of his lands to the resident crofters, who then established the Melness Crofters Estate Ltd. to manage the lands collectively. Despite improvements, problems in land ownership persist. In 1997 two landlords attempted to evict crofters to create a hunting preserve. After much negative media attention, the landlords gave up. The new Scottish parliament is working on legislation that would give all remaining crofters a pre-emptive right to purchase their land when it comes up for sale. The law would also give them time to match outside bids.

Scotland's past continues to shape the politics of the country. In some new and important ways, the past is also the source for a new refashioning of Scottish culture.

A sign welcomes visitors in both English and Gaelic to the Scottish Highland district of Skye and Lochalsh.

4

People and Culture

On a map of northwestern Europe, trace with your finger the rough western edge of the Eurasian landmass. Start at the top of the island of Britain in the Highlands, and move south until you reach the Central Lowlands. Reverse direction, and go north again to include the Hebrides Islands. Move south to the western jut of land known as Wales. Skip over the water of St. George's Channel to Eire, the emerald isle of the Irish, and track the western margin. Jump the water again to include the peninsula of Brittany on the northwest coast of France. You have traced the western outline of a map of Celtic survival. The eastern edge of this region would extend only a few miles inland from the coast.

This sparsely populated fringe of rugged land at Europe's Atlantic margin is an example of an environmental refuge. For centuries the people here have been just beyond the complete control of whatever dominant cultural group controlled the interior portions of Britain and the European mainland. In the case of Scotland, the Gaelic speaking Celts of the Highlands and Western Isles were far from the edicts of Roman conquerors, Scottish kings, and English governments. Hills and poor soils made their land less desirable as a place for development, so the political powers based far to the south tended to ignore them. The Gaelic Scots and their customs are still protected in this natural refuge, although much change has already come. Electronic communication, modern transportation, tourism, and economic development are accomplishing what centuries of political attempts could not.

Today a visitor traveling through the Highlands or the Western Isles will notice dual-language road signs. English place-names and directions are given along with the equivalent information in Gaelic, one of Scotland's two official languages. This part of the country is known as Gaidhealtacht, a linguistic refuge area where the traditional tongue of Scotland may still be heard. Scots Gaelic is closely related to other tongues still spoken in the European Celtic refuge area: Welsh Gaelic in the northwest of Wales, Irish in the western portion of Eire, and Breton in the western part of the Brittany peninsula.

Mainly elderly, most Gaelic speakers are also fluent in English, the other official language of Scotland and the language of most television and radio broadcasts. Linguists and other language scholars worry that not enough young people learn Gaelic. If this trend continues, the language will slowly disappear. Researchers point to steadily dropping numbers. At the turn of the 20th century, 250,000 Scots used the language; today fewer than 65,000 do so. This dramatic decline makes Scots Gaelic an endangered language, like the other Celtic tongues of Europe. Like endangered species, endangered languages are headed for extinction unless steps are taken to preserve them. Disappearing languages are a concern for linguists and others interested in preserving the diversity of world culture and expression. Nationalist politicians are also interested in language preservation— but for somewhat different reasons.

In the case of Scotland, nationalists are leading a revival of Gaelic language and Celtic culture. Instruction in Gaelic is offered at a growing number of schools and colleges in Scotland. In the United States, where many citizens claim Scottish ancestry, the promotion of Gaelic and Celtic heritage is also underway. These trends are part of a broad movement by the Scottish National Party (SNP) and others to revive interest in Scotland's unique identity. The SNP's goal is to gain independence from the UK and make Scotland a sovereign state once again.

Today a visitor to Scotland will find that Scottish culture is being showcased for political reasons. But it is also true that many Scots would be surprised to hear their culture was being "revived," for Scotland is a country where tradition and innovation thrive concurrently.

When Scots sit down to a meal, they are just as likely to tuck in to a traditional dish as they are to eat American-style fast food. Haggis is everyone's favorite example of a traditional Scottish delicacy mainly because of the shock value (at least to some Americans) of the ingredients. Haggis is made with sheep's offal, or entrails, that are boiled, minced, and mixed with oatmeal. This mixture is then sewn into and cooked in a sheep's stomach. Haggis has been eaten for centuries and is still a popular dish. A commercial haggis maker in Edinburgh, Charles MacSween, produces nearly one ton a day for sale in Scotland and the UK and for export. For the squeamish, a contemporary adaptation has been created: vegetarian haggis. Made from black kidney beans, lentils, nuts, mushrooms, and carrots, this version is increasingly popular among Americans celebrating their Scottish ancestry in somewhat diluted form.

Many other traditional foods are still common. Bannocks, or oatcakes, are biscuitlike cakes made with barley and oat

Butcher with haggis in Isle of Skye, Scotland.

flour, baked on a griddle and eaten with cheese. Hotch-potch, or Scottish broth, is a rich stock made with vegetables and mutton or beef. Crowdie (white cheese), black buns made with raisins, and colcannon (a stew of cabbage, carrots, turnips, and potatoes) are still served, especially in smaller towns and rural areas. Scottish salmon is smoked and processed for export, but is also prepared for local consumption in the old style:

smoked over an open fire in a metal box lined with sawdust and sugar.

Scottish beef has long been famous throughout Europe, although the outbreak of hoof-and-mouth disease in the late 1990s and the spread of mad-cow disease in England led to an export ban on Aberdeen-Angus cattle. Another traditional Scottish export item to Europe and the world is what Americans call Scotch. One of Scotland's most dependable exports in terms of demand, Scotch, or whisky, has been produced for centuries. ("Whiskey" is the spelling used in Ireland, the U.S., and some other countries.) People in Scotland rarely call whisky "Scotch." They ask for malt or whisky, or they ask for it by brand name. By law, single-malt Scotch whisky must be at least three years old and must be made in Scotland exclusively from barley malt. Additionally, it must be the product of only one distillery. An important regional distinction is made with the appellation "Highland malt whisky." A malt so labeled must by law originate in the Highlands.

In their social customs the Scottish people keep alive several traditional observances. Hogmanay is the Scottish New Year, celebrated the night of December 31. Traditionally this holiday was far more socially significant than Christmas, which in the past was a low-key private observance. Today Hogmanay is still one of the country's major holidays, although American-style Christmas customs are gaining popularity. The meaning of the word "hogmanay" is somewhat mysterious. Some traditionalists claim it derives from a Gaelic term, *oge maidne,* which means "new morning." Others argue for Anglo-Saxon or Norman French origins. However its origins are explained, today's Hogmanay celebration includes toasting, home visits, fireworks, the lighting of torches and bonfires, and the ritual kissing of strangers.

A celebration with origins much closer in time to our own is Burns Night. Robert Burns (1759–1796) is acclaimed as Scotland's national poet, famous for his lyrics written in the Scottish vernacular. So revered is he that his portrait appears on the Bank of Scotland's five-pound note. His best-known work is written in a northern dialect of English known as Scots. "Auld Lang Syne" is his best-known song— at least outside of Scotland. (Burns purists like to point out that the version sung the world over on New Year's Eve uses a melody different from the one Burns wrote.) Many of his poems and songs are based on folk culture and tales of the Lowlands and Southern Uplands. Today, Scots and people of Scottish ancestry the world over celebrate his birthday, January 25, as Burns Night. By custom Burns Night suppers consist of tatties (mashed potatoes), neeps (turnips), and haggis. The celebration includes readings of "Ode to a Haggis" and some of his other poems, and a speech to the haggis made by one of the participants. Burns is so popular that his birthday was once celebrated in the Kremlin.

If Robert Burns captured the poetic spirit of Scotland's people, then Sir Walter Scott (1771–1832) popularized Scotland's image as a land of heroic adventure and romance. Like Burns, an Anglo-Scot from the southern portion of the country, Sir Walter found in Scottish history and legend the inspiration for his depictions of old Scotland. He was the most popular author of his time, and his novels and histories were translated into dozens of languages. The romantic image of Scotland known the world over is largely the result of his work.

Burns, Scott, and other authors immortalized Scotland's people and customs so successfully that today no other country in the world has such clear, easily identifiable symbols of its national identity. The most famous elements of this identity are the tartans and kilts of the Highlands.

In the United States, "plaid" and "tartan" are inter-changeable terms. But in Scotland a distinction is made between *plaid,* which is the material used for making kilts,

Portrait of Robert Burns (1759-1796), Scottish poet.

and *tartan,* the pattern on the material. Tartans are distinctive checkered patterns, in a variety of colors and designs. Each pattern is called a *sett,* a unique combination of bars of various colors and sizes that intersect at right angles. The clans, or extended families of Scotland, each have their own tartan. The clan system (the term is derived from the Gaelic word for "descendent" or "offspring") was the basis for the political and economic organization of the Highlands for centuries. An informed observer can identify a tartan

Bagpipe players at the Cowal Highland Games in Dunoon.

wearer's clan by "reading" the tartan's design. Today more
than 2,200 different tartans are recognized.

Tartans are usually displayed on kilts, the large blanket that
is pleated around the waist and held in place by a large belt.
Worn in the traditional fashion, the long end of the kilt was
gathered and pinned on the left shoulder. In the past, kilts were
the ordinary dress of workingmen in the Highlands and were
not worn by the wealthy. Now the costume for ceremonial
occasions or, increasingly, as an alternative to standard formal
wear, kilts are unique symbols of Scotland's national identity.
They are part of the formal regimental uniform of several
Scottish and English military units and are worn regularly at

public celebrations, parades, and Scottish national or military observances. An indication of the symbolic power of the tartan and of the deep Scottish immigrant roots in America came on April 6, 1998, when National Tartan Day was declared in the United States. The date was chosen because April 6, 1320, was the signing of the Declaration of Arbroath, a Scottish political document that influenced the authors of American independence.

Another universal emblem of the nation is the bagpipe. Like tartans and kilts, Scottish bagpipes evolved in the Highlands during the 16th to 18th centuries. Sometimes called great bagpipes because of their size and volume, they were adopted by the British military in the 18th century for signaling and marching purposes. Bigger and louder than the uilleann (pronounced 'i-lahn), or elbow, pipes of Ireland or other types of bagpipes found on the continent, Scottish bagpipes are featured prominently in public ceremonies, from the most formal, such as the opening of the Scottish Parliament, to local, informal celebrations and events.

People around the world recognize these cultural elements as distinctively Scottish. They are also reminders to the people of old Caledonia of Scotland's ancient independent spirit and separate nationhood. This spirit and sense of identity are moving the country into a new era of political strength and sovereignty. The "once and future Scotland" is entering the 21st century with a renewed sense of national destiny.

Britain's Queen Elizabeth II in the carriage with Prince Charles and the Duke of Edinburgh ride past the crowd that lines the route along the Royal Mile in Edinburgh, Thursday July 1, 1999. In a colorful ceremony melding populism with ancient tradition, Queen Elizabeth II opened Scotland's first Parliament in nearly 300 years.

5

Nation and State

A visitor to Edinburgh on July 1, 1999, would have seen one of the biggest celebrations in Scottish history. The night before, bonfires and beacon lights lit the sky over the famous hills of the city. In the morning our visitor would have read giant banners and signs hung throughout the city, declaring: "A New Era for Scotland," "A Scottish Millenium," and "A New beginning."

At midday, a parade of 1,500 school children, brass bands, and fife-and-drum corps marched down Edinburgh's oldest street, the Royal Mile. The Duke of Hamilton led a procession conveying the Scottish crown jewels to the Scottish General Assembly Hall. Bagpipes and the famous Scottish army regiments of Argyll and the Sutherland Highlanders accompanied the crown jewels through crowds of people dressed in traditional tartan kilts and dresses. Waiting at the Assembly Hall were distinguished guests from around the world. Once the crown was placed in the hall, Queen Elizabeth II of England officially opened the parliament. To mark the new government's authority, the queen presented Scottish leaders with a specially designed mace, an ancient symbol of power in Great Britain. Dr. Winnie Ewing, the oldest member of the new government, opened the session by saying, "I want to begin with the words that I have always wanted to hear: the Scottish Parliament, which adjourned on 25 March 1707, is hereby reconvened."

Many visitors to Scotland didn't understand the significance of the July 1 celebrations. Didn't Scotland already have a parliament? How could a country as old and prominent as Scotland not have its own government? The explanation for why Scotland's parliament took a nearly 300-year recess is a long story. It involves Scottish and English history, religion, warfare, economic growth, and economic hard times. While Scotland has been a nation for a thousand years or more, it is only since 1999 that it has regained some of the powers of an independent state.

A nation is a group of people with a distinctive culture. Nations may be seen as communities, some large, some small, that are linked by language, religion, and loyalty to a particular region or city. The Scottish people have comprised a nation since the ancient Scots consolidated power over other groups in the northern region of Britain. These groups were the Picts, the Vikings, and the Anglo-Saxons. The Scots came to dominate these groups, and over the centuries a common national identity slowly evolved among them. But for the past 300 years, this nation of Scotland has been a part of the United Kingdom of Great Britain and Northern Ireland (usually referred to as simply the United Kingdom, or UK for short).

Today, Scotland is one of four nations within the UK. Along with the English, the other groups are the Welsh in

Wales and the Irish of Northern Ireland. Until recently the English national loyalty dominated all these other nations. The Scottish people, like the Welsh and Irish, had been pulled into England's economic and political orbit. But— again like Wales and Northern Ireland—Scotland retained a sense of its distinct history and special regional loyalty. Land and life in Scotland are different than in England, and the Scottish people never forgot this difference. "Rise up and be a nation again" is a popular bumper sticker sponsored by a Scottish political party. The slogan reflects the sense of cultural difference kept alive down through the centuries of English rule.

The Long Road to Devolution

The opening of the new Scottish Parliament is an example of *devolution*—a term for breaking up political power and distributing it more widely. The story of Scottish devolution is long and complicated.

In 1707 the Treaty of Union with England merged the existing Scottish parliament with that of England. Economic issues were important in crafting the treaty. One clause in the agreement did away with taxes on products moving from Scotland to England. This created the largest free-trade area in Europe at the time. Scotland and England both benefited from the increase in trade. From the stand-point of the rest of the world, it appeared that Scotland had been absorbed into the UK. During the period 1707 to 1999, the UK Parliament ruled Scotland. Although Scottish voters elected representatives to the UK Parliament, Scotland played a minor role in lawmaking. London, the seat of the UK Parliament, was where almost all-important decisions were made.

Demands for Scottish sovereignty (independent political power) or home rule began in the 1880s. Support for home rule rose and fell over the next hundred years. By the 1960s Scottish

Local people enjoy drinks after voting in the polling station inside the Royal Oak pub in the Scottish village of Urquhart on June 7, 2001.

nationalism had gained popular support, and demands for the restoration of a sovereign Scottish parliament were taken seriously in London. In 1973 a Royal Commission on the Constitution recommended devolution for Scotland. A Scottish Constitutional Convention was established. After years of debate among Scotland's political parties, a devolution bill was written and then put to a popular vote (called a referendum) in September 1997. The Scotland Act passed, and a new era of Scottish nationalism began.

Some Scottish politicians propose breaking the remaining ties with the UK, but a 1999 public opinion poll indicates only 26 percent of Scots favor a complete break with the UK. At least for the time being, its big southern neighbor will continue to play a major role in Scotland's future.

The New Scottish Parliament and the UK Parliament

Layers or levels of government characterize the new Scotland. Two parliamentary bodies now create laws. The new Scottish Parliament deals with domestic issues ("devolved matters"). The old Parliament of Great Britain handles UK-wide issues ("reserved matters"). In some ways this arrangement is like that found in the United States system of federalism. In the United States, political authority is shared among levels of federal, state, and local governments. State governments control land issues, civil law, etc., while the federal government takes care of defense, national security, and international trade.

The benefits of federalism are many. Perhaps most importantly, federalism spreads political power so that no one group or level of government can control a country absolutely. Power sharing among layers is thus more democratic. More levels of government mean that citizens have more representatives working on their behalf. Citizens have more opportunities to participate in government decision making. Local control over most issues is generally desirable and more effective than national control. The closer people are to issues, the more likely they are to deal with them in reasonable and timely ways. This was one of the Scottish nationalists' main arguments in favor of devolution. They said that lawmakers in London simply weren't close enough to Scottish issues and problems to handle them effectively.

The Scottish Parliament's devolved powers include control over health, education, local government, housing, planning, tourism, economic development and financial assistance to industry, most aspects of criminal and civil law, police and fire services, environmental issues, agriculture, fishing, and

Royal Bank of Scotland Group Chief Executive, Sir George Mathewson, poses in front of the Scottish Parliament building in Edinburgh, launching the new Scottish one-pound note.

forestry. The UK Parliament retains control over the "reserved matters": foreign policy, defense, national security, fiscal, economic and monetary policies, energy, and social security.

Scottish citizens now vote for representatives to the Scottish Parliament and representatives to the UK Parliament. Additionally, voters in Scotland also choose representatives to the European Union's Parliament. The European Union (EU for short) is another layer of government. It is increasingly important to the life and well-being of Scotland.

Scotland in the European Union

In addition to enjoying the power and prestige of its new parliament, Scotland is also participating in one of the 21st century's most exciting political and economic experiments: supranationalism. This is a term for the concentration of political power above the level of national governments.

The EU is a supranational organization made up of 15 member countries. These countries have negotiated agreements on free trade, common defense, and even a common currency (the euro). These agreements result in economic benefits for all. But in return, members give up a degree of sovereignty when they join the EU.

Unlike the Scottish or UK Parliaments, the EU is not yet a very democratic organization. The EU parliament has limited powers over lawmaking. Appointed commissioners make EU laws. Despite this flaw, the EU has created the richest free-trade area in the world. It is too early to tell how the new Scottish government will address its role in the EU. The Scottish National Party has said that Scotland needs full independence from the UK to take advantage of its EU membership and benefit fully from EU agricultural and fishery subsidies. Other politicians argue that full independence for Scotland would weaken its position in the EU.

The past few years have been important ones for Scotland. While it has regained its Parliament and a large measure of control over local issues, Scotland is also committed to merging its economic future with that of the EU. A look at Scotland's agriculture and industry helps us understand where Scotland is now and where it may be heading in the years to come.

A weaver with a Harris tweed loom in Harris, Hebrides Islands.

6

Economy

I n Scotland, as we have seen, tradition, adaptation, and innovation exist side by side. While the same might be said of
many other countries, building on the past to create solutions
in the present seems to be a Scottish trait. Particularly when we
look at the economic aspects of Scotland, we see the adaptive
spirit of the nation at work, changing the way people do business
while retaining the best of Scottish heritage. In traditional sectors
such as textile manufacturing or fishing, we see old and new
industrial techniques practiced at the same time. And in the
country's growing high-tech sector, Silicon Glen exemplifies
Scotland's leadership in innovation.

The textile industry has a long history as a mainstay of the
national economy. Today that industry employs about 45,000
people, many of whom work in modern plants producing

garments, hats, gloves, and tents for export to Europe and the United States. Scotland's textile exports topped 700 million pounds in 2000. The U.S.-based WL Gore & Associates represents the new face of the industry. Gore has opened four Scottish production plants in the last four years, all producing the latest in high-tech synthetic materials, such as world-famous Gore-tex.

These modern plants are the latest phase in Scottish textile manufacturing, an activity that began centuries ago as a cottage industry. Cottage industries are traditional rural-manufacturing crafts carried out by individuals working at home. The old cottage trades included shoemaking, weaving, blacksmithing, and milling. Most of these cottage trades are now gone from Scotland, although weavers in the Hebrides still produce world-famous Harris tweed on small locally owned looms. Just as in the early days of the Industrial Revolution, Harris Tweed weaving is farmed out by regional cooperatives to individuals working from home. Finished tweed is crafted locally on the island of Harris or sent to export markets such as the United States, where it is sewn into jackets.

Another example of tradition and adaptability is Scotland's fishing industry, a sector with a centuries-old history. Fishermen still harvest cod, haddock, mackerel, herring, and Norway lobsters using conventional fishing methods. Tough seagoing trawlers, expensive nets, and dangerous all-weather work are hallmarks of North Atlantic and North Sea commercial fishing. But like fisheries worldwide, the Scottish industry suffers from overfishing and stock depletion and faces increasing pressure from international fleets.

One alternative to traditional fishing is aquaculture, or fish farming—the raising of commercially valuable fish in pens or ponds. Since 1990 aquaculture has been adopted in many traditional fishing villages and towns along the north-west coast from the Firth of Clyde north to Cape Wrath, in

Feeding time on a salmon farm. Salmon break the surface of their enclosure as John Ratter, a farmer for Wadbister Salmon Limited, throws them food off the island of Cat Firth in Shetland.

the Outer Hebrides (especially the Isle of Lewis), and in the Orkney and Shetland Islands. Instead of braving the cold waters and winds of the North Sea, fishermen now stay closer to home and raise captive salmon in cages anchored in the numerous saltwater bays, inlets, and channels of the coast. Freshwater cages and ponds are also used to raise rainbow trout. In 2000 some 163 salmon production sites and 44 trout sites as well as 132 shellfish sites (for mussels and oysters) operated in Scotland. Aquaculture seems to be an efficient adaptive solution to the rising worldwide demand for seafood and the growing problem of wild-stock depletions.

Perhaps no other aspect of the Scottish economy illustrates innovation and adaptability as does Silicon Glen, the name given to the area encompassing Glasgow, Edinburgh, Stirling, East Kilbride, and Dundee—the urban heart of the country. Much as 19th-century Scottish shipbuilding on the Clyde developed out of the close proximity of coalfields, steelmaking, and navigable water, Silicon Glen has grown in an area where university research, a major transportation hub, and an educated workforce come together. A large number of companies are sited in Silicon Glen, from hundreds of small locally owned startups to large international corporations such as Sun, Motorola, Agilent, IBM, Microsoft, Oracle, Compaq, and Adobe. The universities of Glasgow, Edinburgh, Stirling, and Dundee produce a highly trained workforce for these businesses. The Artificial Intelligence Applications Institute at Edinburgh University, for example, conducts cutting-edge research into artificial intelligence applications in aerospace, manufacturing, finance, and engineering. Internationally recognized agricultural research institutes are also located in or near Silicon Glen and draw on the expertise of Scottish scientists and technicians.

In important ways, Scotland's economy today barely resembles the old economy of the 20th century. After World War I Scotland suffered a major decline in industries that had been leaders in employment: shipbuilding, steelmaking, and coal mining. From the 1920s until the 1970s, mass unemployment characterized the densely populated Lowlands, near the old hearth of the Industrial Revolution that had made Scotland wealthy in the 19th century. As in other developed countries, a shift from the old industrial economy to the new service economy was under way. Tourism, health, education, insurance, banking, finance, and research and development have now largely replaced heavy industry and manufacturing. During the mid-20th century, Scotland also mirrored another trend found in the developed countries of Europe: a sharp decrease in the number of farm workers. Especially since the 1940s, employment in agriculture has declined significantly. Currently only about 2.5 percent of Scotland's labor force is engaged in farming.

We can generalize about two of the most vital forces changing Scotland's economic landscape over the past half century. The first of these forces is also changing regional economies in many other countries of the world—direct foreign investment, or DFI for short. The impact of the second force is restricted to Scotland, the UK, and other North Sea countries: the discovery of oil in the 1970s.

DFI is the term for the flow of international investment capital from one country to another. In Scotland, investment by foreign-owned companies has steadily gained in importance since the 1940s. North America was then the source of most investment, but lately European and Japanese corporations have been investing in Scottish facilities and research centers. In 1945 only six U.S.-owned manufacturing companies were located in Scotland. By the mid-1980s that number had grown to 181. Currently an additional 138 foreign-owned corporations are producing products and services from a Scottish territorial base. An educated workforce, progressive government, environmental and cultural amenities, and a location that makes Scotland a natural entrepôt to the vast market of the European Union all contribute to Scotland's success in attracting DFI. Today foreign-owned firms directly employ 80,000 people. Almost a third of all manufacturing jobs are with transnational corporations.

Near the top of the list of Scottish growth industries is the field of electronic manufactures. With rapid growth since the late 1970s, this industrial sector now accounts for roughly half of Scotland's total exports. Overseas-based firms operate 158 electronics companies in Scotland, including three of the world's top-ten telecommunications equipment manufacturers—Lucent, Agilent, and Cisco—all of which are based in Silicon Glen. Six global semiconductor plants employ 5,500 people. These operations export primarily to Europe. Nearly 65 percent of Europe's automated teller machines are produced in Scotland, for example. But increasingly exports are headed to other markets, as well. North America and Japan are both now importing Scottish electronics.

The electronics sector in Scotland has a high concentration of production facilities, which are quicker to start up than research-and-development (R&D) centers. A measure of maturity in any industrial field is the size of the R&D sector. R&D operations are more expensive to start up and take longer to make profits. Over time, however, they generate higher returns for investors. A mark of Scotland's progress in developing its electronics sector is that large international investors are moving into Scottish-based R&D. Minebea Company of Japan operates a multimillion-dollar R&D center near Glasgow, where it develops power-control systems. Polaroid Corporation of America operates a design-and-development center at its Vale of Leven plant, developing new products for Polaroid. Cisco Systems is soon opening its first European R&D center in Silicon Glen. This center is planned to be the largest facility outside the United States to develop and test networking software.

Scotland's computer, computer-related equipment, and software sector is also booming. Scotland can boast that more computers are made there per capita (per person) than in any other country in the world. It produces 28 percent of Europe's PCs, nearly 80 percent of Europe's workstations, and 29 percent of the laptops sold in the wealthy European market. Increasingly, computers from Silicon Glen are being exported outside Europe. Currently more than 7 percent of the world's PCs are Scottish made, a figure that will likely rise in the future.

As well as being a major producer of computers, Scotland is now developing a competitive software industry. Investors are attracted to the country's high quality of life and political stability, plus its closeness to European and North American markets. More than 800 software companies are now located there. Some are among the world's giants in software development and services: HP, Compaq, Sun, IBM, Cisco, and NCR. But most are small- and medium-sized enterprises that employ fewer than 50 people each. An impressive 82 percent of these companies are independent or headquartered in Scotland; most rely on domestic sales in the UK. But significant changes are taking place within this industry that will broaden its world reach. A recent development in software sector investment is in Scottish-based software R&D. These software R&D companies create and test new services and products. As this trend continues, Silicon Glen's share in the lucrative global software market will continue to grow.

Overall, the information and communication technology industry accounts for about 15 percent of Scotland's gross domestic product—more than three times the figure for the tourism industry. Almost half of this sector provides software services or applications, and 22 percent provide software products.

In a related area of telecommunications, Scotland has attracted over 200 call centers in the last 10 years. These operations employ over 46,000 people. Extensive market research indicates that the Scottish accent is the most acceptable and understandable form of English worldwide. As a result, giant corporations such as Microsoft and Morgan Stanley–Dean Witter have sited their first overseas call centers in Scotland. Nearly a third of these centers also offer services in languages other than English, a testimonial to the high quality of Scotland's educational system.

The financial service sector is a more recent growth area. Several large international financial institutions, including J. P. Morgan Chase and the Bank of Bermuda, have located their technical development teams in Scotland. As in other areas of foreign investment, these companies are attracted by the world renown of Silicon Glen. But competition from nearby regions is intense. Other growing financial centers in nearby Dublin and Copenhagen share many of Scotland's cultural and environmental amenities. They also boast of highly trained workforces and their progressive politics. Competition with these and other European cities for DFI will surely increase in the future.

Energy from the North Sea

November 11, 2001, was the 25th anniversary of oil and gas production in the North Sea area known as the Brent field. Located 116 miles (187 kilometers) northeast of Lerwick, Shetland Islands, the Brent field is the scene of some of the largest offshore drilling platforms in the world. Built to withstand the harsh North Sea climate, these platforms withstand winds of more than 100 miles (161 kilometers) per hour and sea surges of 100 feet (30 meters) or more. Technically sophisticated, they use the latest drilling technology, such as multi-lateral and sidetrack wells. The four major platforms in the field stand in waters approximately 460 feet (140 meters) deep. Each is 900 feet (274 meters) high from seabed to flare stack with well depths of over 8,500 feet (2,590 meters). By the end of 2001, Brent was producing almost 10 percent of all gas and oil consumed in the UK. The cost of deep-well drilling and high-tech platforms means that North Sea oil is expensive. But because of its proximity to high-energy consuming markets, it is a major source of energy for Europe and one of the world's key non-OPEC oil regions.

Aerial view of an offshore oil platform owned by the Total Oil Company in the seas off Scotland.

Discovery of oil and gas in the North Sea revitalized the economy of the Orkney and Shetland Islands and the cities of the northeast. Inverness, Scotland's largest northern city, now specializes in the manufacture and repair of oil platforms. Aberdeen, an old northeast fishing center, is the maritime oil industry's primary service center. Further south along the coast, Edinburgh's port of Leith, once important in the fishing and shipbuilding industries, is now a center for North Sea oil drilling and pipeline equipment. Major oil and gas pipelines run from production fields offshore to Cruden Bay north of Aberdeen. Other lines extend from northern North Sea fields to the Orkneys and the Shetlands.

Production in 2000 exceeded 6 million barrels a day, a record for the region. But the North Sea is considered "mature," meaning it is unlikely that major new fields will be discovered or developed there. Despite the projected decline in oil production over the next decade, natural-gas production is growing while demand is on the rise worldwide. Because of its proximity to European markets, North Sea gas will be a significant fuel in the coming years. Some pipelines are already in place, and hungry consumers in Germany and elsewhere are already buying gas from Scottish waters.

Not only does North Sea oil and gas fuel European cars and cooking stoves, but it also fuels nationalist political sentiment in Scotland. Since the discoveries of the 1970s, the Scottish National Party (SNP) has claimed the North Sea reserves as rightfully belonging to Scotland. An SNP bumper sticker from a few years ago read: IT'S OUR OIL. If full political independence comes in the future, a newly independent Scottish government would run largely on North Sea oil and gas revenues. Economic estimates indicate that if Scotland received 80 percent of UK's North Sea oil, Scotland's GDP would rise by 22 percent, and GDP per capita would rise above that of the UK. That 80 percent figure is based on the

United Nations Convention on the Law of the Sea that establishes a system for drawing sea boundaries between countries. If the Law of the Sea's "equidistance rule" is applied to draw sea borders between an independent Scotland and England, then Scotland *would* get most of the oil.

Traditional industries, DFI, and oil have combined to create new wealth and well-being in Scotland. But as we will see, the effects of the new economy are felt in some places more than in others. As modern as the Scottish economy is, some areas, such as the Western Isles, remain as they have been for many generations.

The British nuclear reprocessing plant at Dounreay in Scotland.

CHAPTER

7

Regional Contrasts

Scotland's new economy has not taken root in all regions. The Hebrides, the Highlands, and the Northern Isles are all far from the digital domain of Silicon Glen. In sharp contrast to the Lowlands, most parts of the North—such as the Orkneys, the Shetlands, and the Western Isles—have no foreign-owned manufacturing plants. Other areas, such as Argyll and Bute in the northwest, have fewer than three.

At the broadest level of regional contrast, we might begin by dividing Scotland into three broad demographic and economic territories. These areas correspond roughly to the three physical divisions of Scotland. North of a line from the headlands of Fife Ness on the eastern coast to the Sound of Jura on the west coast is a region called the Gaelic North. Home of most traditional Scottish culture, this portion of the country is primarily rural and has far fewer people than the south, which contains most of Scotland's population. The largest urban areas are located in the central belt, or waist, of the country—what we will call the Urban Lowlands. In this relatively small region live more than half of Scotland's 5 million people. In the far south lies the Border country, the part of Scotland closest to England. Accents and lifestyles here resemble those of northern England, so we might call this region the Anglo-Scottish south.

Before we look at these three territories in more detail, we should gain an overview of Scotland's demography and the trends that influence population change.

In 1975 Scotland's political divisions were reorganized. The old county organization was dismantled and the country was divided into administrative regions. The regions, their areas, and administrative cities are listed in the table on page 71.

Most recent population change in Scotland, as in other places in the world, can be attributed to changing economic conditions. For example, every year since 1860 large numbers of Scottish workers left home for economic opportunity in North America and Australia. Many of these emigrants were among Scotland's best-educated and most highly trained elite who could not find employment in the country. This so-called brain drain peaked during the period from 1920 to 1970. Since the 1980s, however, the trend has reversed; today more people are moving to Scotland than are leaving, an indication of Scotland's economic boom.

A more recent example of change is in Strathclyde, which has lost population steadily since 1971. It that year nearly half of Scotland's people lived in or within a few miles of Glasgow. Today about 44 percent of Scotland's total population lives in this area, but with 2,286,000 people, it is still the country's population center. As Scotland's old industrial heartland, Strathclyde suffered severe economic downturns beginning in the 1920s. Only in the last few years has the regional economy begun to improve.

Name	Area Sq. miles (Sq. km)	Population (1993)	Administrative City
Regions			
Borders	1,814 (4,698)	105,300	Newtown St. Boswells
Central	1,017 (2,634)	272,900	Stirling
Dumfries and Galloway	2,481 (6,425)	147,900	Dumfries
Fife	509 (1,318)	351,200	Glenrothes
Grampian	3,358 (8,697)	528,100	Aberdeen
Highland	9,806 (25,398)	206,900	Inverness
Lothian	662 (1,715)	753,900	Edinburgh
Strathclyde	5,214 (13,504)	2,286,800	Glasgow
Tayside	2,893 (7,493)	395,200	Dundee
Island Areas			
Orkney	377 (976)	19,760	Kirkwall
Shetland	553 (1,432)	22,830	Lerwick
Western Isles	1,119 (2,898)	29,410	Stornoway

Table 1: Area, Population, and Administrative City by Region and Island Area

Areas of population and economic growth include Lothian, Grampian, Tayside, and Central. These administrative regions are all located in the Lowlands or on the narrow eastern coastal portion of the country. Grampian's growth is directly related to

Glasgow city chambers in George Square.

the North Sea oil development of the 1970s. The city of Aberdeen in particular has added many relatively high-paying energy-related jobs to its economy. So successful, and lucky, has Aberdeen been in making the transition from a regional fishing and agricultural center to Scotland's premier oil town that it now has the highest per capita gross domestic product (GDP) in Scotland, along with Lothian.

Looking at economic trends and population change is an important way to understand Scotland's regional differences, but perhaps the most important contrast is in the distribution of wealth. As well as being the location of Scotland's two largest cities, the Urban Lowlands region accounts for most of the country's economic productivity.

The variation in affluence between north and south is dramatic. The Highlands and Islands are the poorest places in Scotland. In this region most people rely on seasonal employment in relatively low-paying tourism related jobs or they work small crofts or in the fishing industry. It is no surprise that the lowest GDP per capita is found in the north. Compounding the problem of low pay is the fact that country living is more expensive. A recent study funded by the Scottish Parliament indicates that the cost of living is generally higher in rural areas than in cities and that the lowest average weekly earnings were all in the countryside. As Scotland's economy has grown in the past 30 years, the gap between richest and poorest regions has widened.

The Gaelic North

High-tech industry and foreign investment have not altered the economy or touched the lifestyle of people in the north. In villages on Lewis or Harris, two of the largest Western Isles, daily life appears little changed from a hundred years ago. Fishermen still trap lobsters for export to London and Paris and fish for haddock or cod, or they tend salmon in new aquaculture operations. A few farmers work crofts as they have for generations. Weavers produce Harris Tweed for export to North America. But with a lack of new opportunities and the lure of high-paying jobs in the south, many young people today are leaving the north, just as they have for the last several generations.

The entire Highland region, including the administrative city of Inverness has a population of less than 207,000,

Exterior of Scottish thatched cottage.

although in terms of area—more than 9,800 square miles (2,500 square kilometers)—it is Scotland's largest administrative unit by far. The North of Scotland has never had as many people as the south. During the industrial revolution, growth of the textile industry prompted the depopulation of many northern estates for conversion to sheep pasture. In 1800 approximately 377,000 sheep were raised in the Highlands; by 1880, estimates placed the number at over two million. During this same 80-year period, the human population dropped by 200,000. Almost all of these people were victims of forced removal. Some immigrated to North America; many others moved to the rapidly growing cities of the Lowlands or to England.

Shortly after the worst years of the Highland removals, the Gaelic North became the scene of another less violent confrontation. With the construction of rail lines in the late

19th century, the sparsely populated Highlands became a tourist destination. So quickly were large numbers of visitors drawn to the rural north that by the 1890s residents began to debate the value of tourism. Critics claimed that railroads were responsible for the extinction of bird and animal species. Their basic argument was that tourists were "loving the country to death." This debate goes on wherever tourism is an important part of the economy. Today the Gaelic North is a low-key tourist destination. Many crofter cottages have been converted to weekly or monthly rental properties for foreign visitors. Bed-and-breakfast accommodations are increasingly popular, as well. Tourism here is small-scale and appropriate to the rural beauty of the region.

As in the Western Isles and Highlands, tourism is important to the northern archipelagos, the Orkneys and the Shetlands. One important difference between these isles and the rest of the north is that much of the North Sea's oil production takes place 150 to 200 miles (240 to 325 kilometers) off Scotland's northeastern coast. Fishing and crofting are still practiced in the Orkneys and in the Shetlands. Daily life is similar to the Hebrides in most ways, although the oil industry has brought a few high-paying jobs over the last 20 years. Young people are not leaving in the numbers they once were. But oil experts predict a decline in North Sea oil production over the next 10 years or so, and this situation may change. Crofts and fishing, along with tourism, will once again become the staple activities of the Orkneys and Shetlands.

The Urban Lowlands

Lothian (along with Grampian) has Scotland's highest per capita GDP. One of the smallest administrative units in terms of area at only 662 square miles (1,715 square kilometers), this region is the wealthiest in Scotland. Much of the Lowlands economic success may be accounted for by the "multiplier effect." This term describes the creation of jobs as new investors or manufacturers move into developing areas. One of the key attractions for new investors in Scotland is that suppliers and related supporting businesses are already in place in the Lowlands. The area has an efficient transportation system and is close to UK and EU markets. Major universities in the area produce some of the world's most highly trained and well-educated graduates. The rich cultural heritage and the environmental amenities of Scotland are additional draws for investors and workers alike. It makes sense for new businesses to locate in such a region because they can take advantage of existing services and transportation development. Every new high-tech export-related job creates a ripple in the local economy, generating jobs in the expanding service sector.

Roughly one-third of Scotland's total manufacturing employment is in foreign-owned plants, and the majority of these are in the Lowlands. As we have seen, the benefits of foreign investment are spread unevenly in the country. But so, too, is a direct dependence on the global economy. A survey of the number of jobs in foreign owned industries points to a potential problem in the economic future of the Lowlands. Corporate restructuring or shifts in global demand could create big changes in local employment. Business decisions by managers in North America or Japan might result in plant closings in Fife, where 7,450 people work in the foreign-owned sector, or in South Lanarkshire (9,100 jobs) or West Lothian (8,750 jobs). These areas are dependent on the global fortunes of transnational corporations. Altogether, about 81,750 people in Scotland are employed in 330 foreign-owned manufacturing plants. All of these workers are part of the economic, political, and cultural phenomenon known as globalization. In dramatic contrast to the fishermen, crofters, and weavers of the north, their working careers are tied to corporate decision makers far away.

A worker at the massive IBM plant in Greenock goes to work.

As well as being the economic engine of Scotland, the Urban Lowlands region is home to the largest cities in the country. Glasgow developed early in the Industrial Revolution as a manufacturing and shipbuilding city. As those economic sectors went into a sharp decline in the 20th century, Glasgow suffered from high unemployment and from urban blight—the lack of maintenance and abandonment of buildings—and urban flight—the movement of people away from poverty-stricken inner cities. Glasgow has recovered from the bad old days of the 1960s and 1970s. The East End district was refurbished in the 1980s and the city has begun to attract new investment.

Overview of Edinburgh.

Only about 40 miles (65 kilometers) away, Edinburgh is a dramatically different urban area. In the 18th century it was known as the Athens of the North, a cultural center that rivaled London. In contrast to Glasgow's reputation as Scotland's industrial and shipbuilding center, Edinburgh was the country's intellectual center, with a world-famous university and a distinctive urban architecture. Founded as a defensive stronghold and with a skyline still dominated by Castle Rock, Edinburgh's Royal Mile is renowned for its historical buildings. One end of the Royal Mile is anchored by Edinburgh castle. At the other end is the Palace of Holyroodhouse, the residence of Mary, Queen of Scots.

The Anglo-Scottish South

The southernmost region of Scotland is the Border country. In the long struggle between England and Scotland this region was often a no-man's land, famous for its outlaws. Today largely an agricultural region, Scotland's ancient past is still visible on the land. The ruins of four 12th-century abbeys, along with the famous Roman walls, still stand in the midst of farmlands and small towns. Sir Walter Scott is buried near the Gothic ruins of Dyrburgh Abbey. According to legend, the cedars and yew trees around Dyrburgh were planted by returning Crusaders. With a population of just 105,000, the bucolic Border country is dramatically different from the bustling Lowlands just a little ways to the north.

An unidentified man with a Scottish flag wrapped around him walks home
after voting.

Future of Scotland

S cotland in the 21st century is the scene of two political trends found in other parts of the world: devolution and supranationalism. What is unique about Scotland is how these trends are intertwined.

As we saw in our survey of the country's history, Scottish independence vanished in the Act of Union with England in 1706. Although Scotland lost its parliament and a great degree of its sovereignty, it grew wealthy on North American trade and became England's economic partner in the early years of the Industrial Revolution. Union worked out to be in the best interests of both countries. As global forces began changing the United Kingdom's economy after World Wars I and II, and the UK joined the European Economic Community (now the European Union, or EU) in 1973, the advantages of partnership with the English were not as obvious as they had been. The Scottish National Party (SNP) and others argued that Scotland's relationship with the EU was more important for the future of Scotland than membership in the UK. "Rise Up and Be a Nation Again," an SNP slogan emblazoned on auto bumper stickers, captures the revivalist spirit of the movement for independence. Many young people in Scotland are attracted to the SNP message, which is popularized by celebrities such as Sean Connery.

Also fueling the nationalist movement in the 1970s was the discovery of oil off Scotland's northeast coast. Although North Sea energy production is expected to decline in the coming years, Scotland has developed the infrastructure to support continued oil and natural-gas exports to European markets. With independence could come as much as 80 percent of the North Sea oil revenues that now go to the UK. As exciting as the possibilities of independence are, it seems unlikely that England will quietly allow Scotland to claim the lion's share of what remains of the North Sea energy wealth. Nevertheless, the SNP sees the reopening of the Scottish Parliament as the first step on the road to complete independence.

While the SNP and other nationalists focus on Scotland's devolution, others are exploring the possibilities that supranationalism offer to the country.

The EU is the most successful (and peaceful) attempt in history to create an economic and political organization made up of sovereign states. Fifteen European countries are members of the EU, and plans are underway to expand membership in the next few years. Together these states have created the single richest market in the world.

Scotland is represented in the EU governing institutions as a member of the UK. It currently has no independent status, but by participating in the regional development programs of the EU, Scotland is finding that it has much to gain by strengthening its European or EU identity. The EU's principle of subsidiarity supports the Scottish argument for further devolution of political power. The subsidiarity principle is that decision-making should be done at the local and regional level if possible; only if local government cannot solve a problem should national governments step in. This suits the arguments for independence that nationalists have made for years: Who better to solve local problems than local leaders?

Not only does the EU encourage local political decision making, but also its approach to regional development gives Scotland a new source of development money. The poorest regions of Scotland have for several years been receiving money from the European Regional Development Board (ERDB). The ERDB disburses funds to EU areas that lag behind in terms of measures such as gross domestic product per capita or per capita incomes. Local environmental initiatives, community development, and tourism industries also receive EU money. In addition, the European Social Fund provides resources for training and education in areas eligible for structural fund spending.

The Gaelic North, other rural areas, and even some declining industrial areas in Strathclyde have benefited from these EU structural programs. The far north in particular has recently been the target of EU development spending. With less than 75 percent of EU's average per capita income, the Highland region, along with the islands, was granted Objective 1 status—meaning that it was a top priority for rural development funds. In March 1999 the EU determined that this status would soon be lifted, although additional money would be allocated for the next few years.

Scotland's future, then, lies somewhere between the old union with England, Wales, and Northern Ireland and a broader union with all the countries of Western and Northern Europe. The great experiment of supranationalism will continue to bring the states of the EU closer together, forging new ties of interdependence and, perhaps, a new supranational identity for Europeans. At the same time,

A European Union flag flutters at the Sint-Pietersplein in Gent, Belgium. On
October 18, 2001 the European Union's Informal Summit took place under
Belgian presidency.

devolution in the UK will allow the Scottish people to build a new sense of independence and nationhood. How these two interconnected forces shape Scotland's future will be fascinating to watch. What we can say with certainty is that the people of Scotland will hold onto their unique identity and culture in the new world of the 21st century, whatever political trend prevails—just as they have for the last thousand years.

Facts at a Glance

Land and People

Official Name Scotland

Location Western Europe, northern portion of island of Britain.

Area 30,414 square miles (77,174 square kilometers), slightly smaller than Maine.

Climate Marine West Coast

Capital Edinburgh

Other Cities Glasgow, Aberdeen, Inverness

Population 5,114,600 (2000, est.)

Major Rivers Tay, Spey, Clyde, Tweed, Dee, Don, and Forth

Major Lakes Loch Lomond, Loch Ness, Loch Awe

Mountains Grampians, Cheviot Hills

Official Languages English, Scotch Gaelic

Religions Presbyterian, Anglican, Roman Catholic

Literacy Rate 99% (1978 est.)

Average Life Expectancy 75 years

Economy

Natural Resources Oil, coal, arable land

Agricultural Products Sheep, cattle, potatoes, barley, oats, fish

Industries Electronics, information systems, defense, semiconductors, office machinery, data processing equipment, whisky, oil and gas

Major Imports Machinery, chemicals, food, consumer goods

Major Exports Computers, computer-related products, office machines, wool, whisky, textiles, software products

Major Trading Partners European Union, U.S., Canada, Japan

Currency Pound sterling

Government

Form of Government Constitutional monarchy

Government Bodies Scottish Parliament (Edinburgh); UK Parliament (London)

Formal Head of State British Queen or King

Head of Government Prime Minister

Voting Rights All citizens 18 years of age and older

296	First mention of Picts in Roman literature.
368	Pict, Scot, and Saxon tribes attack Romans in London.
843	Kenneth MacAlpin unites Scots and Picts.
1295	The Auld Alliance—a mutual defense treaty—signed between Scotland and France.
1296	Scotland annexed by England. Scotland's Coronation Stone—the Stone of Destiny—removed to Westminster Abbey by Edward I of England.
1314	Robert the Bruce defeats Edward II's English army at the Battle of Bannockburn.
1411	University of St. Andrews founded.
1451	University of Glasgow founded.
1559	Scottish Reformation begins, led by John Knox.
1582	University of Edinburgh founded.
1603	James VI of Scotland becomes James I of England – Union of the Crowns.
1642	Civil War in England.
1682	National Library of Scotland founded.
1695	Bank of Scotland founded.
1707	Scotland formally united with England in the 1706 Act of Union, forming the United Kingdom. Scottish Parliament votes itself out of existence.
1715	First Jacobite rebellion.
1744	The Honourable Company of Edinburgh Golfers founded (world's first golf club).
1760s	The period known as the Highland clearances begins.
1768	First edition of the *Encyclopedia Britannica* published in Edinburgh.
1826	Scotland's first railway opened between Edinburgh and Dalkeith.
1830s	Clydeside, near Glasgow, becomes site of UK's premier shipbuilding industry.
1913	Clydeside ship production peaks and enters period of slow decline.
1950	Stone of Destiny stolen by Scottish nationalists from Westminster Abbey. By tradition, English monarchs sit on the stone while being crowned. When it is recovered, some people claim it is a copy.
1967	The last of the Clydebank passenger liners, *Queen Elizabeth II*, is launched.
1975	The first oil from the North Sea is piped ashore at Peterhead.
1996	The Stone of Destiny returned from London to Edinburgh Castle.
1997	UK passes the Scotland Act, enabling the devolution of power from London to Scotland.
1999	Scottish Parliament reconvened after 292 years.

Further Reading

Margaret Aitken, 2001. *In My Small Corner: Memoirs of an Orkney Childhood.* Scottish Cultural Press.

Caroline Arnold, 1997. *Stone Age Farmers Beside the Sea: Scotland's Prehistoric Village of Skara Brae.* Clarion Books.

Robert Burns: The Scottish Bard (Illustrated Poetry Series) Gramercy Press. 1999.

A.D. Cameron, 2001. *Discover Scotland's History.* Scottish Children's Press.

Danny Hann, 1986. *Government and North Sea Oil.* Palgrave.

Andrew Hargrave, 1985. *Silicon Glen: Reality or Illusion? A Global View of High Technology in Scotland.* Mainstream.

Francis Jarvie, 1996. *The Romans in Scotland.* Seven Hills Books.

Robert Orrell, 2000. *Blowout.* Sheridan House.

Dwayne Pickels, et al., 1997. *Scottish Clans and Tartans (Looking into the Past).* Chelsea House.

Jane Porter and Date Wiggins, eds., 1991. *The Scottish Chiefs.* Atheneum.

Eric Richards, 2000. *The Highland Clearances.* Birlinn Ltd.

Sir Walter Scott, 2001. *From Bannockburn to Flodden: Wallace, Bruce, and the Heroes of Medieval Scotland.* Cumberland House.

Sir Walter Scott, 2001. *From Glencoe to Stirling: Rob Roy, the Highlanders, and Scotland's Chivalric Age.* Cumberland House.

Holly Wallace, 2001. *The Mystery of the Loch Ness Monster.* Heineman Library.

Duncan Williamson, 1998. *Tales of the Seal People: Scottish Folk Tales.* Interlink Pub Group.

Basic print references:

Merriam Webster's Geographical Dictionary (third edition) 1998. Springfield: Merriam-Webster, Incorporated.

Goode's World Atlas (19th edition) 1995. Rand McNally.

Internet-accessed references:

CIA World Factbook 2000. Country Listing for United Kingdom *[http://www.odci.gov/cia/publications/factbook/index.html]*

U.S. Energy Information Administration: North Sea Fact Sheet. *[http://www.eia.doe.gov/emeu/cabs/northsea.html]*

Scottish Technology Industry Monitor, Royal Bank of Scotland: Survey of information and communications technologies industry in Scotland. *[http://www.royalbankscot.co.uk/economics/press_articles_presentations/stim.pdf]*

Silicon Glen: general background and business overview. *[http://www.siliconglen.com/]*

BBC Online: In Search of Scotland (history). *[http://www.bbc.co.uk/history/scottishhistory/]*

The Scottish Office: Department of Agriculture. *[http://www.scotland.gov.uk/agri/documents/ais-00.htm]*

The Scottish Parliament. *[http://www.scottish.parliament.uk/]*

Index

Index

About the Author

ROGER DENDINGER was born in New Orleans and grew up there and in Mobile, Alabama. He lives with his wife and three sons—Zac, Nash, and Gabe—in the Black Hills. He is a professor of geography at the South Dakota School of Mines and Technology.